PRINCIPLES
of
EDUCATION
教育原理

Dedicated to parents, educators, learners,
and leaders of the universes

獻給所有父母，老師，學生，和領袖們

Donald W. Sung

宋武峰

Donald W. Sung 宋武峰

Acknowledgments

致謝

I am very grateful for the guidance and mentorship of

Dr. George E. Forman

and

Dr. Charles J. Sung.

throughout my study and in the preparing and writing of this book on childhood education.

Many thanks to the people who have educated or influenced me in my pursuance of educational study, especially

非常感謝喬治福爾曼博士

宋查爾斯J博士

在我學習過程中，

以及準備和寫作這本兒童教育書籍的過程中，

給我指引與輔導。

Prof. Tom Chiaromonte

Prof. Ala Samarapungavan

Prof. Helen Patrick

Prof. David Sears

Prof. Katheryn McGuthry

Dr. Shian-jung D. Chen

Prof. Monica E. Lee

and

Dr. James J. Sung.

非常感謝在我攻讀教育的旅途中

教導我或影響我的人，

特別是

湯姆‧基亞羅蒙特教授

阿拉薩馬拉蓬文教授

海倫‧帕特里克教授

大衛‧西爾斯教授

凱瑟琳‧麥格思裡教授

陳献忠博士

莫妮卡E. 李教授

和

詹姆士 J. 醫師

Many thanks to people who have supported and contributed to the writing of this book, especially

Peggy C. Wong

Michael Kelso

Diana Chu

Shelly Dowden

Allen Tsai

Lisa D. Wang

Robert Treister

Zerlina Wong

Paul Nicholson

Ginnie Lo

and

Barbara Scott.

非常感謝支持和貢獻本書寫作的人們，

特別是

佩吉・C・黃

邁克爾・凱爾索

戴安娜朱

雪莉・道登

艾倫蔡

麗莎・D・王

羅伯特・特里斯特

澤琳娜黃

保羅・尼科爾森

金妮羅

和

芭芭拉・斯科特。

Donald W. Sung 宋武峰

Preface

前言

The human brain and the human body are very complicated, and so is human education. This book presents a childhood educational theory with a system of principles of a learner's conditions, environment, and educational processes.

人的大腦和身體結構非常複雜，因此人的教育也不容易一蹴可幾。本書介紹一套兒童教育理論，它是根據和學習者自身條件、生長環境以及學習過程有關的各種原理所發展出來的一套思想體系。

The system recognizes that a child's intelligence, emotions, and social interactions continue to develop in tandem with his growth and bio-physical conditions. This is a system with dynamic principles, such as the time factor principle, the pursuance of betterment principle, and the latency in a person's change of

physical and mental state principle. These principles may vary with time and should be applied in tandem with the changes in the learner's condition as well as his learning environment.

這個思想體系考慮到孩子的智力、情感以及人際關係會隨著他的成長和生理狀況的變化而不斷同時發展。它的原理常常是動態的，如時間因素原理、追求改善原理、人的身心狀態變化潛伏期原理等。這些原則可能會隨時間而變化，應與學習者狀況和學習環境的變化同步推出應用。

The system attends to the negative impacts and other side effects of an educational process. These unwanted side effects may accumulate and cause potential difficulties and problems in the future.

該系統關注教育過程的負面影響以及其他副作用。這些不必要的副作用可能會累積
並在未來造成潛在的困難和問題。

Education impacts a child throughout his life, which is why this system presents principles, such as maintenance stage principle and conflict resolution principle, that may be consistently applied throughout children's lives.

教育會影響孩子的一生，這就是為什麼該系統提出的原則，例如維持階段原則和衝突解決原則，可
以應用在孩子的一生中始終如一。

More than one principle in the system may be applied to a learner's situation. An effective guidance may be created by applying a combination of these principles.

可以同時應用系統中一個以上的原則以應付學習者的情況。可以通過應用這些原則的組合來創建有效的指導。

The principles are divided into three groups: learner's state (functions and conditions), learner's interactions with environment, and introducing a learner to the world. These principles are interdependent. Hopefully the readers may internalize and combine them into a complete educational theory.

這些原則分為三組：學習者的狀態（功能和條件），學習者與環境的互動以及引導學習者踏入社會。這些原則是
相互依存的。希望讀者可以將它們內化並組合成一個完整的教育理論。

Donald W. Sung, J.D., M.B.A.
May 25, 2022

宋武峰 (唐納宋) 法學博士/企管碩士
2022 年 5 月 25 日

Contents 目錄

Part I - Learner's State 第一部 – 學習者的狀況

1. Body Function Curve Principle
身體功能發展原理

Each body part or condition has its own function curve.

每個身體部位或狀況都有它們自己的功能發展曲線。

Corollaries to Body Function Curve Principle
身體功能發展曲線原理的推論

   A. A person's heart functions vary with the time.

   人的心臟功能會隨時間而變化。

   B. A newborn baby first learns to breathe, then learns to drink.

   剛出生的嬰兒先學會呼吸，然後才學會喝奶。

   C. A newborn baby spends most of his time and energy in growth and rest.

   新生嬰兒大部分時間和精力都花在成長和休息上面。

D. During infancy, a baby learns how to use ears, eyes, arms, legs, and the rest of the parts of his body.

人類在嬰幼兒期間，學習如何使用耳朵、眼睛、手臂、腿和身體的其他部位。

2. Gross Capacity Principle

整體能力原理

A person's gross capacity varies with time, physical and mental state, and his environment.

一個人的整體能力會隨時間、身體與心理狀況、以及他所處的環境而改變。

Corollaries to Gross Capacity Principle
整體能力原理的推論

A. A person's gross capacity is limited.

一個人的整體能力有限

B. A person's gross capacity may be reduced by fatigue and increased with a proper rest.

一個人的整體能力會因為疲倦而降低，也會因為得到充分休息而增加。

3. Free Capacity Principle

可供自由使用的能力原理

A person's free capacity is the difference by deducting the person's committed capabilities from his gross capacity.

一個人可供自由使用的能力指的是他的整體能力扣掉他先前運用所剩的能力。

4. A Person's State Principle

個人狀況原理

A person's state at any point of time is the accumulation of the person's conditions in all dimensions, or areas, including but not limited to the person's physical and mental conditions, educational background, experiences, the surrounding environment, connections, and communications with other people.

一個人在某一時刻的個人狀況指的是他在各方面或各領域條件的總和，包括但不局限於他本人的身體與心理條件、教育背景、經歷、周遭環境、人際關係以及跟別人的溝通情形。

Corollaries to Person's State Principle
個人狀況原理的推論

A. Physical illness may affect a person's learning, depending on the toll of the illness on the person and on the subject matter to be learned.

身體疾病可能會影響一個人的學習，影響多大要看該疾病對他的損傷程度
以及他所欲學習的科目性質而定。

B. Positive existing knowledge may help a person's learning, the effectiveness of which depends on the direction, depth, lapse of time, and other relevant factors regarding the existing knowledge.

一個人現有的正面知識可幫助他的學習。是否有效就要看現有知識的方向、深度、
學習間隔時間以及其他因素而定。

C. A person's relationship with family or community members may affect that person's learning positively, negatively, or in a way of partially positive in some dimensions and partially negative in other dimensions.

一個人與家人或鄰居的關係會對他的學習有正面的、負面的影響或者某些方面有正面影響，而其他方面則有負面作用。

D. A person's state is different from one another's, and his state changes from time to time.

一個人的狀況不同於他人的狀況，而個人的狀況會隨時間而異。

5. Potential of a Person Principle
個人學習潛力原理

A person's potential for learning at any point of time depends on the intended target, the suitability of the information available, the transmission of the information, and the state of the person.

在任何時間點一個人的學習潛力會依學習要達成的目標性質，能取得的資訊是否合適，該資訊的傳輸是否理想，以及個人的狀況是否良好而定。

6. Learning and Physiology Correlation Principle
學習與生理相關性原理

Learning correlates with a person's physiology.

學習與個人的生理現象互有關聯。

Corollaries to Learning and Physiology Correlation Principle
學習與生理相關性原理的推論

A. A person's sense organs input information for learning.

一個人透過感覺器官輸入學習所需的訊息。

B. The information inputs into a person's short-term Memory.

訊息先傳輸到個人的短暫記憶。

C. The information is organized and stored into a person's long-term Memory.

訊息經過整理後才會儲存到個人的長期記憶。

7. Trammel State Principle
阻礙狀態原理

To effectively educate a person who is in a trammel state, an educator must find out the causes of his being in the trammel state and the body functions affected by the trammel state.

要能有效教育一個處於受阻礙狀態的人，教育者必須找到阻礙他的原因，以及他受到阻礙的身體功能。

Corollaries to Trammel State Principle
阻礙狀態原理的推論

A. When a student's learning is handicapped by nearsightedness, the trammel state can often be removed by wearing a pair of eyeglasses.

當一個學生的學習因為近視而受到阻礙時，通常讓他戴近視眼鏡就可能移除此一阻礙。

B. When a student's learning is handicapped by loss of hearing, the trammel state can often be removed by wearing a pair of hearing aids.

當一個學生的學習因為聽力喪失而受到阻礙時，此一約束狀態通常在讓他戴助聽器之後就可能移除。

C. When a toddler's reluctance to learn number counting is due to his belief that "math is hard," an educator may avoid using the word "math" and take another occasion to show him how to count cookies or something the toddler is interested in.

如果一個學步中的兒童因為相信「算術很難」而不願意學習，教導他的人可以的話就要避免用「算術」這個字，利用機會給他示範如何數餅乾或者能引起這個小孩子興趣的東西。

8. Principle of Physical and Mental State Co-Relationship
身體與心理交互作用原理

A person's physical state may change with a change in his mental state, and vice versa. There exists a relationship between a person's change in physical and mental state.

一個人的身體狀況會因為心理狀況改變而跟著改變，反之亦然。一個人的身體與心理狀況的變化存在一種互相影響的關係。

9. Principle of Latency in a Person's Change of Physical and Mental State
一個人的身體與心理狀況改變的潛伏期原理

There is a time delay for a person's physical state to change due to a change in mental state, and vice versa.

一個人的身體狀況隨著心理狀況改變所產生的變化時間上會有延緩的情事。反過來也一樣。

10. Dominant State Principle
顯性狀態原理

A person's dominant state varies with time, existing physical and mental state, and his environment.

一個人的顯性狀態會隨時間、既有的身體與心理狀況、以及他所處的環境而改變。

11. Recessive State Principle
隱性狀態原理

A person's recessive state varies with time, physical and mental state, environment, and becomes noticeable in the absence of an overshadowing dominant state.

一個人的隱性狀態會隨時間、身體與心理狀況、以及他所處的環境而改變；在缺乏強勢的顯性狀態時，隱性狀態就會比較明顯。

12. Critical State of Existing Knowledge Principle
知識臨界點(關鍵點)原理

When a person reaches and exceeds the critical state of his existing knowledge, he may recognize the retained input information, learn from it, and organize it into a newly organized information.

當一個人的知識達到且超越某一臨界點(關鍵點)的時候，他就會有能力在留存的輸入資訊中辨認出值得學習的，加以學習,整理成比較有系統的新資訊。

Corollaries to Critical State of Existing Knowledge Principle
知識臨界點(關鍵點)原理的推論

    A. When an athlete reaches his critical state of existing knowledge regarding muscle control, the athlete may improve his performance.

    當一個運動員控制肌肉的知識達到某一臨界點(關鍵點)的時候,他就可以改善他的運動表現。

    B. When a musician reaches his critical state of existing knowledge regarding muscle control and musical understanding, the musician may improve his performance.

    當一個音樂家控制肌肉的知識和對音樂的了解達到某一臨界點(關鍵點)的時候,他就可以改善他的音樂造詣。

    C. When a student reaches his critical state of existing knowledge with respect to a course, the student may progress in the study.

    當一個學生對某個科目所擁有的知識達到某一臨界點(關鍵點)的時候,他的學業就會精進。

13. Information Management Principle
資訊管理原理

A person may use his capacity to manage his information input in all or part of the follow ways:
一個人可以透過下列所有或部分的方式利用他的能力來管理他所收到的資訊:

    I. ignore the information;

    不理會剛進來的資訊;

    II. place the information in a temporary memory;

    將新進來的資訊暫存在臨時記憶;

    III. preliminarily interpret the information;

    初步解讀該筆資訊;

    IV. discard some of the interpreted information;

    將解讀過的部分資訊丟棄;

    V. retrieve existing knowledge;

    擷取已有的知識;

    VI. compare the retained information to the existing knowledge;

    將留下來的新資訊拿來和已有的知識比較;

    VII. filter or discard the retained information;

    過濾或丟棄留下來的新資訊;

    VIII. recognize patterns in the retained information;

    辨認留下來新資訊的格式;

    IX. apply preset routine associated with the pattern if the retained information is in the existing knowledge;

    如果留下來的新資訊已經是已有知識的一部份,就動用與該資訊格式相關的預定例行步驟加以處理;

X. organize the retained information into a useful newly organized information if the retained information is not in the existing knowledge; and

如果留下來的新資訊還不是已有知識的一部份，就將留下來的新資訊整理成比較有系統的有用資訊

XI. store the newly organized information into the person's long-term memory.

並且將新整理出來的資訊存入個人的長期記憶。

Corollaries to Information Management Principle
資訊管理原理的推論

A. Information which does not belong to information inputs is ignored by the recipient.

接收者可以將不屬於進來訊息的資訊加以忽略。

B. The retained information, unless incorporated into the long-term memory, will disappear in the future.

留下來的資訊如果沒被納入長期記憶儲存起來，將來自然就會消失。

C. The newly organized information may be incompatible with or contradict the person's existing knowledge.

新整理出來的資訊有可能跟學習者已有的知識不能相容或互相矛盾。

D. The person may modify his existing knowledge and incorporate all or part of the newly organized information into that existing knowledge.

他可以修訂已有的知識，然後將新整理出來的資訊全部或部分納入為已有的知識。

E. The person may also discard or reject the newly organized information due to its incompatibility with his existing knowledge.

他也可以因為新整理出來的資訊與舊有的知識不一致而將它丟棄或予以拒絕。

F. When a child doesn't know how to join other children's play, he may play by himself, observe, and learn until he feels comfortable to communicate with other children.

當一個小孩不知道如何加入其他小孩一起玩，他可以自己玩、在旁邊觀看、學習，直到他覺得
跟其他小孩溝通不會覺得不自在。

G. A child learns information pieces first, before he learns the relationship between these pieces.

小孩子先學習零碎的資訊，後來才能夠學會這些個別資訊之間的關係。

H. A child may learn causes and effects between information pieces after he has opportunities to learn all necessary pieces of information.

小孩子要先有機會學習所有需要的零碎資訊，然後才能習得這些零碎資訊之間的因果關係。

I. It may take less learning capacity for a person to learn from information previously organized by other people.

一個人學習別人已經整理出來的資訊有時候可能比較不費力。

J. Children often learn from mistakes.

小孩子常常能從錯誤中學習

14. Ideal Education Principle

理想教育原理

If the state of a person and the potential of a person are known, it is possible to create a process for an ideal education.

如果知道一個人的狀況跟他的潛能，替他創造一個理想的教育過程是有可能的。

Corollaries to Ideal Education Principle
理想教育原理的推論

A. At the first meeting with a client, a lawyer needs to assess his client's legal position, i.e., the relevant facts, the applicable laws, and the potential consequences the client may encounter, to formulate a strategy to help the client.

律師跟他的客戶第一次見面時，需要評估客戶在法律上的處境，意即有關的事實，可能引用的法律條文，以及該客戶可能要承擔的後果，如此律師才能夠找出可幫忙他客戶的訴訟策略。

B. When meeting with a patient, a physician needs to review history of his patient, examine the patient, and/or run laboratory tests to make a diagnosis, i.e., assess the state of the patient and, if necessary, review the patient's records. With the diagnosis and prognosis, the physician will be able to prescribe a treatment plan.

醫師跟他的病人見面時，他需要回顧病人的病史，替病人檢查，有必要的話讓病人進檢驗室檢查，如此醫師才能夠做初步的診斷，意即評估病人的身體狀況，有必要的話參考病人的病歷，有了診斷以及預後評估，醫師才能提出治療的方案。

C. An educator needs to know his student's level, potential, and educational goals. With such knowledge, the educator will be able to design the most appropriate curriculum for his student.

教育者需要知道學生的程度，潛能和教育的目標，有了這些知識，老師才能為他的學生設計最合適的課程。

15. Pursuance of Betterment Principle

追求更好原理

If there are options, a person will choose the one which seems to be the better choice for him or her.

如果有得選擇，一個人會選取對他或她似乎比較好的方案。

Corollaries to Pursuance of Betterment Principle
追求更好原理的推論

A. People often find benefits in planning their tasks.

人們通常從預先策畫他們的工作而得到利益。

B. People often find benefits in living in a society.

人們通常從生活在社會上與人交往而得到利益。

C. People often find benefits in peace and avoidance of unnecessary conflicts.

人們通常從保持平和與避免無謂的衝突而得到利益。

D. People often find benefits in education.

人們往往從受教育得到利益。

E. Babies often practice motor movements.

　　嬰兒經常練習運動身體各部位。

F. Toddlers often enjoy imitative play.

　　學步中的孩童經常模仿別人的行動而樂在其中。

G. Artists are often motivated by ways to improve their painting.

　　畫家常常因為找到方法使他們能改善畫作而得到鼓舞。

H. Musicians are often motivated by ways to improve their performance.

　　音樂家常常因為找到方法使他們能改善演奏而得到鼓勵。

I. A person may be his own educator.

　　一個人可以成為他自己的教育者。

16. Motive Principle
動機原理

A person uses his capacity for what he sees fit.

人會盡力去做他認為合適的事情。

Corollaries to Motive Principle
動機原理的推論

A. A person may enjoy reclining to rest, seeking safety, fulfilling needs, improving environment, having better performance, becoming a better person, or acquiring better personality traits.

　　一個人可能會享受躺下來休息，尋找安全感，滿足需求，改善環境，讓自己表現更好，當個更好的人，或者習得更好的人格特質。

B. If newly organized information is unfamiliar to a person, he may want to find out whether the information will have a good or bad consequence.

　　一個人如果對新整理出來的資訊不熟悉，他也許會設法弄清楚該筆資訊是否會產生好的或不好的影響。

C. A newborn baby cries when he feels hungry.

　　新生兒肚子餓了就會哭。

D. A baby cries when he feels that is the only way for him to communicate.

　　當新生兒覺得哭是他唯一的溝通方式時，他就會哭。

E. When a child is attracted to something interesting, he may want to learn more about it.

　　當小孩子受到某個有趣的東西吸引的時候，他就會想要知道更多跟它有關的事情。

F. A child may be guided to discover a new motive.

　　小孩子的行為也會為了發現新的動機的引導。

17. Desire Principle
渴望原理

A person may wish to have something which is not currently in his possession, or he may wish to have someone else's services.

一個人會希望擁有某個他目前沒有的東西，他或許也會希望得到別人的服務。

18. Motivation Principle
驅策力量原理

A person is inclined to act when there is a strong motive to do so.

當一個人有強烈的動機做某件事，他就會有付諸行動的傾向。

Corollaries to Motivation Principle
驅策力量原理的推論

A. A person may be motivated by needs.

一個人也許會受到需要的驅策。

B. A person may be motivated by desires.

一個人也許會受到慾望的驅策。

C. A baby's motivation for milk is reduced after feeding.

一個嬰兒餵過奶之後，驅策他喝奶的力量就往下降了。

D. A person may be motivated by external rewards.

一個人也許會受到外在報酬的驅策。

E. External rewards may lead to positive or negative motivation.

外在報酬會引導出正面或負面的驅策力。

F. A motivation may contain multiple motives and varies with time.

驅策行動的力量也許包括多個動機，且會隨時間而改變。

G. Proper guidance may motivate a learner.

適當的引導或許能激勵學習者。

19. Action Principle
行動原理

A person may take an action when he has the necessary capacity and is motivated to do so.

一個人有需要的本事，以及足夠的動機，就有可能採取行動。

Corollaries to Action Principle
行動原理的推論

A. A professional is motivated to work efficiently and may create an effective way to handle routine or similar tasks.

專業人員會鞭策自己做事要有效率，也會找出有效的方法處理日常的工作或類似的任務。

B. When a person is motivated to do multiple tasks, he may have to arrange the order or sequence of the tasks, or prioritize them.

當一個人受到驅策要完成多項任務時，他也許必須先安排好那些工作的先後順序，決定孰先孰後。

C. When the tasks are beyond a person's capacity, he may have to let go of some tasks, or he may not complete them.

當那些任務超越一個人的能力範圍的時候，他也許必須放棄部分任務，或者可能完成不了。

20. Self-Sufficiency Principle
自給自足(不用依賴別人)原理

A person in a state of self-sufficiency has a motive to act at will.

達到自給自足(不用依賴別人)境界的人就能夠有動機根據自己的心願行動。

Corollaries to Self-Sufficiency Principle
自給自足(不用依賴別人)原理的推論

A. The feeling of self-sufficiency may yield confidence for what the person is about to act.

自給自足(不用依賴別人)的感覺會讓人對即將採取的行動有信心。

B. A state of self-sufficiency varies with time.

自給自足(不用依賴別人)的心理狀態會隨時間改變。

C. A self-sufficient person may encounter newly organized information which may impact positively or negatively on his feeling of self-sufficiency.

自給自足(不用依賴別人)的個人有可能遇到新整理的資訊，讓他自給自足(不用依賴別人)
的感覺受到正面的或負面的衝擊。

D. The feeling of self-sufficiency is one of the reasons why a person does not feel the need to communicate with other people.

自給自足(不用依賴別人)的感覺是使一個人不覺得有必要跟別人來往的主要原因之一。

E. A child may play by himself alone when he doesn't know how to join other children's play.

一個小孩子如果不知道該如何加入別的小孩子一起玩耍的時候就可能選擇自己玩。

F. Self-sufficiency may be a motivation for learning.

自給自足(不用依賴別人)的心理狀態可能會驅動自己學習。

G. A person may or may not like to communicate with other people when he reaches a self-sufficiency state.

當一個人達到了自給自足(不用依賴別人)的心境，他可能會也可能不會願意跟別人溝通(來往)。

21. Confidence Principle
信心原理

A person feels confident when he believes that all necessary resources and capabilities needed for a particular task is fully under his control, directly or indirectly.

一個人如果認為他已經能夠完全直接地或間接地掌控要完成某一特定任務所需的所有
資源和能力，他就會覺得有信心。

Corollaries to Confidence Principle
信心原理的推論

A. A person's confidence is based on the dominant state of his existing knowledge.

一個人的信心建立在他現有知識是否位居主宰地位的基礎之上。

B. A person's confidence may change with newly organized information.

一個人的信心會隨新整理的資訊而改變。

22. Principle of Comfort Zone
舒適圈原理

A comfort zone is a situation when a person is confident that he will be safe and without stress.

舒適圈指的是讓一個人覺得他自信自己處於很安全又沒有壓力的狀況。

Corollaries to Comfort Zone Principle
舒適圈原理的推論

A. A child may feel comfortable to play by himself when he doesn't know how to join other children's play.

一個小孩子如果不知道怎麼跟其他小孩玩在一起，他可能自己玩才覺得比較自在

B. A person's comfort zone may change with newly organized information.

一個人的舒適圈會因為新整理的資訊而改變。

C. New information may bring motives for a person to leave his comfort zone.

新資訊可能會給予一個人動機離開他的舒適圈。

23. Effect of Education Principle
教育效果原理

The effect of education is determined by the appropriateness of source information, the fidelity in transmission, and the acceptance by the recipient.

教育是否有效取決於學習資源是否適當，教導是否盡責，以及受教者是否能接受。

Corollaries to Effect of Education Principle
教育效果原理的推論

A. An imperfect education may create unintended impacts on the learners.

不完美的教育可能會對學習者造成預期不到的衝擊。

B. A less than appropriate education may create positive, negative, or mixed impacts on the learners.

未盡適當的教育可能會對學習者造成正面的，負面的，或互相抵觸的衝擊。

C. Prior negative learning may impede the effectiveness of the current education.

以前負面的學習經驗可能會妨礙當下教育的效果。

D. Physical disorder, imperfect or less-than-appropriate prior education, or a combination of these factors may cause a learning disorder.

身體的缺陷，以往不完美或未盡理想的學習經驗，或者這些因素的組合可能會造成不正常的學習。

24. Act in Time Principle
及時行動原理

An event must take place in a particular time and environment to cause a particular impact.

一個事件要能產生某一特定作用跟它發生的時機與場合有密切關係。

Corollaries to Act in Time Principle
及時行動原理的推論

A. An untimely education may miss the window of opportunity for learning.

未能及時教育將會錯過學習的時機。

B. Learning from an information input which is not connected with the learner's existing knowledge is less effective.

所收到的資訊如未能與學習者現有知識有關，學習效果就會比較差。

C. To provide effective guidance, an educator needs to know the state of the learner.

教育者必須知道學習者的狀況才能提供效果比較好的指導。

D. Time is of the essence of early childhood education.

時間是兒童早期教育成功的要素。

25. Limited Resources Principle
有限資源原理

A person realizes that he does not have unlimited resources.

一個人應該了解他並沒有無窮盡的資源。

Corollaries to Limited Resources Principle
有限資源原理的推論

A. When a person's information input comes to near temporary memory capacity, he may experience shortened temporary memory or loss of memory on some recent events.

當一個人所收到的資訊量接近他的短暫記憶的容量，他的的短暫記憶有可能受到壓縮，或者他會喪失對某些最近事件的記憶。

B. When a person retrieves a lot of long-term memory into temporary memory, he may experience shortened temporary memory or loss of memory on some recent events.

當一個人擷取部分長期記憶到他的短暫記憶，他的的短暫記憶有可能受到壓縮，或者他會喪失對某些最近事件的記憶。

C. When a person faces too many factors to consider at one time, he may consider only some of the factors.

當一個人一時間要面對思考太多因素，他或許只能將其中部分納入考量。

26. Relevant Factors Principle
相關因素原理

A person considers only a subset of factors which may also be limited by the person's resources.

一個人一時只能認真思考受到資源限制而縮減考量的因素的一部分。

Corollaries to Relevant Factors Principle
相關因素原理的推論

A. When schooling is no longer relevant to the student's needs or goal, a student may consider dropping out of the school.

當上學唸書跟一個學生的需求與目標不再相關時，他可能會想到退學不唸了。

B. A marketer may consider how, when, where, and to whom an advertisement should be targeted to maximize its probable impact on the target audience.

一個市場開拓者會考慮應該如何，何時，在哪裡，針對哪個客戶群推出某支廣告，才能
對廣告對象造成最大的可能影響。

27. Learning Path Principle
學習途徑原理

Learning path is a relevant factor to the effectiveness of a person's learning.

學習途徑是一個與一個人學習效果有關的因素。

Corollaries to Learning Path Principle
學習途徑原理的推論

    A. An educator often finds that the sequence of his teaching material presentation impacts students' learning.
教育者常常發覺呈現他的教材的順序會影響學生的學習。

    B. It could be effective for a person to learn from information previously organized by other people.
一個人學習別人以前整理過的資訊會比較有效果。

28. Priority Principle
優先順序原理

If a person wants to do several things and it is better to do one thing at a time, then he will create an arrangement in accordance with the order of his preferences.

如果一個人要做好幾件事，他也知道最好一次只做一件，那麼他就會根據他喜好的次序安排工作的順序。

Corollaries to Priority Principle
優先順序原理的推論

    A. When a student has one week to study for final exams on multiple subjects, he may decide which subject to study first, second, etc.

當一個學生有一個星期的時間準備許多科目的期末考，他會決定先唸哪個科目，其次哪一個等等。

    B. When a new patient is rushed into an emergency room, a triage team and/or ER doctor may decide which injury or condition has the highest priority and requires immediate treatment, and which will be next, etc.

當一個病人剛被推進急診室，分科小組和/或急診室醫師會決定哪一個損傷或狀況需要最優先處理，立即治療，其次是哪一個等等。

29. Time Factor Principle
時間因素原理

Time is always a relevant factor.

時間一直都是相關的因素。

Corollaries to Time Factor Principle
時間因素原理的推論

    A. Teaching science today is totally different than it was in the early 19th century.
現在教科學跟十九世紀早期的科學教育完全不一樣。

    B. A military plan will have to be modified to reflect changing circumstances in a war, such as new and/or unanticipated developments.

為了反映瞬息萬變的戰況，譬如有新的，意想不到的發展，軍事行動計畫必須一直修正。

C. A person's existing knowledge varies with time.

一個人現有的知識會隨時間而改變。

D. Some long-term memory may vary with time.

有些長期記憶也會隨時間而改變。

E. The dominance of some long-term memory may decrease with time.

有些長期記憶的主宰局勢也會隨時間而改變。

30. Knowledge Accumulation Principle

知識累積原理

A person's existing knowledge is an accumulation of all educations received and adjusted with the changes in time.

一個人現有的知識是他所受的教育以及隨著時間改變而所做的調整累積而成的。

Corollaries to Knowledge Accumulation Principle
知識累積原理的推論

A. Advanced education is appropriate to learners who have accumulated sufficient existing knowledge.

對累積足夠已有知識的學習者而言，高等教育很合適。

B. An educator may provide bridging education to learners who do not have sufficient existing knowledge for an advanced education.

一個教育者可以提供銜接教育給沒有足夠可接受高等教育的已有知識的學習者。

C. There is no age limitation for the constant changes in a person's existing knowledge.

對一個人已有知識不停改變來說，沒有年齡的限制。

31. Personal Condition Principle

個人狀況原理

A student's personal condition (e.g., health, physical condition, and psychological issues) affects his ability to learn.

一個學生的個人狀況(如健康，身體狀況，以及心理問題)影響他的學習能力。

Corollary to Personal Condition Principle
個人條件原理的推論

An educator should consider his learner's physical condition in planning the learner's curriculum and workload.

教育者在規劃學習者的課程與學業負擔時，應該考量他的學習者的身體狀況。

Part II - Learner's Interactions with Environment
第二部 學習者與環境的互動

32. Environment Principle
環境原理

Environment is a relevant factor in education.

環境是一個與教育有關的因素。

33. Trust Factor Principle
信賴因素原理

When a person believes or finds thru experience that a particular source of information is reliable and/or beneficial, he may trust that information source. Conversely, if a particular source of information is seen or experienced as unreliable and/or detrimental, he may distrust that source.

當一個人相信或從經驗中發現某一特定資訊來源很可靠,且/或有助益的,他就會信賴該資訊來源。反過來,某一資訊來源被視為或給人不值得信任的經驗,且/或會造成傷害的,那他就不會信賴它。

Corollaries to Trust Factor Principle
信賴因素原理的推論

A. Trust factor relates to a person's existing knowledge.

信賴因素與個人已有的知識有關。

B. Trust factor correlates with a person's capacity in accepting a new information input.

信賴因素和一個人接受新進來資訊的能力互相關聯。

C. A person's self-trust on a particular matter correlates with his self-confidence.

一個人自認為某一特定的事值得信賴和他的自信有相互關聯。

D. A person's trust in an educator correlates with his learning capacity.

一個人之所以信賴一個教育者跟他的學習能力有相互關聯。

E. Trust is a factor in association with another person.

信賴就是一個人和另一個人交往的重要因素。

F. Educational environments, including but not limited to parents, siblings, relatives, friends, school, church, communities, associations, society, government, and the broader world correlate with a person's trust in them.

教育環境，包含卻不侷限於父母、兄弟姊妹、親友、學校、教會、社區、聯誼會、社區、政府和更廣大的世界，與一個人是否信任他們有有相互關聯。

G. The length of time in negotiation and resolution of a conflict correlates with the parties' trusts in one another.

透過協商解決某個衝突所需要花的時間跟所有的當事人是否互相信賴有相互關聯。

H. Mutual trusts are built upon mutual positive educations and eliminations of negative existing knowledges.

互相信賴建立於互相之間的正面教育，並且能消除已有的負面認知。

I. Foundation of a lasting peace is built upon the trusts of all parties.

持久的和平乃奠基於所有相關人員之間互相信賴。

34. Critical State for Learning Principle

學習的關鍵狀況原理

A person's critical state for learning varies with time.

一個人學習的關鍵狀況隨時間而改變。

Corollaries to Critical State for Learning Principle
學習的關鍵狀況原理的推論

A. When a baby needs sleep, he is too tired to learn.

當一個嬰兒需要睡眠時，他就是太疲倦不適合學習。

B. A person in pain may not reach the critical state for learning.

痛苦中的一個人可能尚未進入學習的關鍵狀況。

35. Window of Opportunity for Learning Principle

學習機會窗口原理

A person or group's window of opportunity for learning varies with time.

一個人或一個群體的學習機會窗口隨時間而改變。

36. Dwindling Window of Opportunity for Learning Principle

學習機會窗口逐漸變小原理

A new window of opportunity for learning dwindles with lapse of time.

隨著時間的逝去，一個學習機會窗口會逐漸變小變窄。

Corollaries to Dwindling Window of Opportunity for Learning Principle
學習機會窗口逐漸變小原理的推論

A. Through passage of time a learner becomes tired or distracted, and the window of opportunity for learning may be gone.

隨著時間過去，一個人會變累容易分心，他的學習機會窗口可能就會消失。

B. A party's window of opportunity for learning is diminishing with the approaching of deadline.

一群人的學習機會窗口會因為工作期限的逼近而逐漸變小。

C. A student's window of opportunity for learning decreases along with the decrease of his free capacity.

一個學生的學習機會窗口會隨著他的可用能量的減少而逐漸變窄。

37. Development of Learner's Potential Principle

學習者潛能發展原理

There exists a sequence of ideal educations which may be infinitely close to a targeted potential of a learner.

可能有一系列理想的教育機會無限接近一個學習者的目標潛能。

Corollaries to Development of Learner's Potential Principle
學習者潛能發展原理的推論

A. A learner's state is often not in a perfect educational condition.

一個學習者的狀況常常並不符合完美的教育條件。

B. The targeted potential of a learner is often measured without a perfect condition.

一個學習者期望達成目標潛能的評估常常不見得是在完美的條件下完成的。

C. If a sequence of ideal educations are aimed toward a learner's targeted potential, and one ideal education is followed by another more effective ideal education, then the sequence is moving closer and closer to the learner's potential.

如過一系列的理想教育是朝向一個學習者期望達成目標潛能推進，而且一波更有效率的理想教育又緊接著一波理想教育推出，那麼這一系列的教育肯定越來越能發揮學習者的潛能。

D. As conditions of an educational sequence approach perfect conditions, the sequence may be infinitely close to the potential of a learner.

當一系列的教育逐漸接近理想的條件的時候,該系列就會無限接近一個學習者潛能的發揮。

E. If a biased condition is used in a sequence of development of a potential learner, then the result of the development process is unpredictable.

如果一個潛在學習者的發展過程中順應了一個偏差的條件,那麼這個發展過程的結果就無法預期。

38. Education Priority Principle
教育優先順序原理

The process of an education is conducted in accordance with priority principle.

教育過程理應根據優先順序原理來推展。

Corollaries to Education Priority Principle
教育優先順序原理的推論

A. The priority conditions often change with time.

優先順序條件常常隨著時間而改變。

B. An educational process often changes when there is a change in priority conditions.

每當優先順序條件有了變化,教育過程通常也會改變。

C. Many students have higher energy at the beginning of a class, and their ability to learn declines after a long class.

許多學生在開始上課的時候精神奕奕,上課時間長了他們的學習能力就會往下降。

D. It may be better to have a break between two classes.

課堂之間應當下課休息比較好。

E. It may be better for a student to take a short break before starting another long self-study.

一個學生在另一段長時間的自習開始之前,應當短暫休息一下比較好。

39. Bond Principle
人際關係原理

A simple bond relationship is unilateral.

一個單純的保持距離關係往往只是單方面的。

40. Distancing Principle
保持距離原理

A simple distancing relationship is unilateral.

一個單純的保持距離關係往往只是單方面的。

Corollary to Distancing Principle
保持距離原理的推論

A party may distance itself from another party whether the other party has a bond with him or not.

不管當事一方是否自認為與另一方有關係,對方仍有可能與之保持距離。

41. Family Tie Principle
家庭關係原理

A family tie is a combination of a person's multiple bond relationships and multiple distancing relationships with members of the person's family.

家庭關係指的是一個人和他的家庭成員之間的多種人際關係和多種保持距離關係的總和。

42. Family Education Principle
家庭教育原理

A person receives education from family members all the time.

一個人不管甚麼時候都從他的家庭成員得到教育。

Corollaries to Family Education Principle
家庭教育原理的推論

   A. A family provides environments for members to learn from one another.

   一個家庭提供其成員之間互相學習的環境。

   B. Family bonds are often created through family education.

   家庭中的人際關係常常是由家庭教育所造成的。

   C. A disagreement between two family members provides an education for all members.

   兩個家庭成員不和睦對所有的成員都是一種教育。

   D. A family often provides children with educational programs, such as schooling, private tutoring, sport programs, etc.

   一個家庭常常提供小孩子教育活動項目，譬如上學，家教，體育活動等。

43. Total Education Principle
全面教育原理

A person constantly receives educations from available information.

一個人隨時不斷地從他所接觸的資訊得到教育。

Corollaries to Family Education Principle
全面教育原理的推論

   A. A person often learns from information in his environment.

   一個人常常可以從環境中的資訊學習到東西。

   B. A person prioritizes learning from available information.

   一個人會安排如何學習可用資訊的優先順序。

   C. A child may be alert to, and will learn from, new information, either taught or untaught.

   一個小孩子可能會對新的資訊，不管是否來自老師的教導，有警覺心，也可能學習到東西。

   D. A child can be influenced by his surrounding environment, including family, neighborhood, school, church, friends, media, and so on.

   一個小孩子會受到周遭的環境，包括家人、鄰居、學校、教會、朋友，媒體等，的影響，

44. Connection Principle
關聯原理

Connection is a relevant factor in education.

關聯是教育的重要因素之一。

Corollaries to Connection Principle
關聯原理的推論

    A. A person becomes attached to an organization when he forms a connection with the organization, or with at least one of the organization members.

      當一個人與一個組織或組織中至少一位成員產生關聯，他就與該組織有某種聯繫。

    B. A person becomes attached to a church when the person forms a connection with the church or with a church member.

      當一個人與一個教會或教會中的某位成員產生關聯，他就與該教會有某種聯繫。

    C. A student connects to a school when he registers to study in the school.

      當一個學生到一間學校註冊，他就對該校產生歸屬感。

45. Attachment Principle
親近感原理

Attachment is created by prior experience.

先前的情感經驗會產生親近感。

Corollaries to Attachment Principle
親近感原理的推論

    A. A child may not want to separate from the person he is attached at the first day of school.

      一個小孩子可能不會要和他上學第一天就比較親近的同學分開。

    B. Attachment may help or distract a person from windows of opportunities for learning.

      親近感可能有助於掌握，也可能會讓一個人錯過學習的機會窗口。

46. Transmission Principle
傳播原理

A transmission of information is a special type of education process.

資訊的傳播是教育過程的一種特別形式。

Corollaries to Transmission Principle
傳播原理的推論

    A. A marketing campaign is a special type of education.

      行銷活動是一種特別的教育方式。

    B. Interactive teaching is a communication between teachers and students.

      互動教學強調老師與學生之間的溝通。

C. Misinformation may cause a positive, negative, or neutral education, or a combination of various educations.

傳播錯誤的訊息會造成正面的，負面的，或中性的教育，或者不同種教育的混合。

47. Imperfection Principle

不完美原理

Education often occurs under imperfect educational conditions.

在不完美的教育條件下，教育仍然照常發生。

Corollary to Imperfection Principle
不完美原理的推論

Perfect conditions appropriate to a learner in all dimensions rarely exist.

適用一個學習者所有方面的條件都很完美的情形非常少見。

48. Education Limit Principle

終極教育原理

One goal of an education is the limit or end of the education.

教育的其中一個目標就是將教育推到極限或到達教育的終點。

49. Approaching an Education Goal Principle

接近教育目標原理

It is possible to find an ideal education sequence that is infinitely approaching the goals of the education.

找到一個理想的教育進程，使能無限接近教育目標，是有可能的。

Corollaries to Approaching an Education Goal Principle
接近教育目標原理的推論

A. An education can be more effective if at least some of the relevant conditions are appropriate conditions.

如果至少有些相關條件的適用性都很洽當，這一項教育就可能比較有效果。

B. If every ideal act of education in a sequence is followed by another more effective ideal act of education, then the sequence may approach closer and closer to its goals of education.

如果尾隨一系列教育的每個理想的行動就是另一個更有效率的教育行動，那麼該系
列就有可能逐步接近教育的目標。

C. If the conditions of an education sequence approach a Perfect Condition, the sequence may approach infinitely close to the goals of the education.

如果一系列教育的條件傾向接近完美的狀況，那麼該系列就可能無限接近教育的目標。

D. If a biased condition is used in approaching an education goal process, the result of the educational process is unpredictable.

如果在逐步接近教育目標過程中運用了有偏差的條件，教育過程的結果就很難預料了。

50. Principle of Tool

工具原理

The effectiveness of an educational tool varies with educators, learners, time, and environments.

教育工具是否有效會隨著教育者，學習者，時間與環境的變化而改變。

Corollaries to Tool Principle

輔導原理的推論

    A. It may be beneficial to adjust a tool with respect to the educator, the learner, the environment, and time frame.

        助教可以解釋問題給提出問題的學生聽。

    B. A tool may be less effective or create unintended consequences in education.

        一件工具也有可能沒那麼有效，或者會造成不預期的教育後果。

51. Principle of Guidance

輔導原理

A guidance may lead to positive or negative learning. A positive guidance may be achieved by providing proper assistances.

輔導可能導致正面的或負面的學習。提供適當的幫助就能達成正面的輔導。

Corollaries to Guidance Principle

輔導原理的推論

    A. A teaching assistant may explain problems brought by students.

        助教可以解釋問題給提出問題的學生聽。

    B. A teaching assistant may guide a student to study a particular section in the textbook.

        助教可以指引學生去讀教科書的特定章節。

    C. Guidance might include, but is not limited to, understanding a targeted person as well as the goals and implications of the targeted education; observing the targeted person; preparing curriculum; and communicating with the targeted person.

        輔導可能包括，但不限於了解某特定人員以及特定教育的目標與意涵；觀察特定人員；
        準備課程；以及和特定人員溝通。

    D. A negative guidance may lead to a negative education.

        負面的輔導可能造成負面的教育。

    E. An inappropriate guidance may lead to inappropriate or unintended education.

        不洽當的輔導可能導致不洽當或沒預期到的教育。

    F. A good guidance takes into consideration various dimensions of the learner now and in the future.

        一樁好的輔導會將學習者現在以及未來的所有不同方面的問題都納入考量。

    G. Guidance varies with the person targeted by it.

        輔導會隨著輔導對象的不同而改變。

H. Guidance, as well as its targeted person and goals of education, varies with time.

輔導，還有輔導的特定對象與教育的目標，都會隨時間而改變。

I. Organizing information for effective learning is a guidance tool.

為了得到有效學習而整理資訊就是一種輔導的工具。

J. Dividing a larger amount of information into smaller pieces of information, suitable for a learner's free learning capacity, is a guidance tool.

將大量資訊分割成較少的資源，使符合學習者可資運用的學習能力，就是一種輔導的工具。

K. Arranging the order of a sequence of the input information may be a guidance tool.

將接收到的一系列的資訊按順序安排好，可能就是一種輔導的工具。

Part III - Introducing a Learner to the World
第三部 引領學習者踏入現實世界

52. Group Principle

群體原理

A group functionality is an integration of its members' functionality. Human existence depends on groups.

群體的機能是個別成員機能的總和，人類的存在需要仰賴群體的存在。

Corollaries to Group Principle

群體原理的推論

    A. Every individual will die, but his group may survive.

        每個個人都會死去，但是他所屬的群體可能繼續存在。

    B. An isolated person must work extremely hard to provide his own food, clothing, shelter, etc.

        一個孤立的個人必須非常努力的工作才得以滿足他自己的飲食，穿著，遮蔽等需求。

    C. It is very difficult for an isolated individual to make scientific advancement.

        一個孤立的個人很難推動科學的進展。

D. A family can provide living necessities, guidance, and education to family members.

　一個家庭的成員能夠提供生活需要，輔導，以及教育給其他家人。

E. A family can provide external connections to other people and groups.

　一個家庭可以提供成員對外界人士與群體的聯繫。

F.　Each person in a group is unique.

　一個群體的每個人都是獨一無二的。

G. The difference in skills among the members of a specific people group is observable.

　一個特定人群的成員技術才能的差異是有目共睹的。

H. When one person finds out that another person possesses a tangible or intangible property of his critical need, there is a motivation for him to calculate whether he can obtain that property.

　當某個人發現有另外一個人擁有他急於需要的某種有形或無形的資產，他就會有
　動機去盤算是他可取得該一資產。

I.　When two members in a group mutually discover that the other has something which can satisfy his critical need, there is a motivation for a trade.

　當一群體中有兩個人互相發現對方有東西能夠滿足自己的緊急需求，那他們
　兩人就會存在有進行交易的動機。

J.　A society is formed when members of people groups find out they can benefit from an integration of their groups due to trade and economic of scale.

　當許多人群的成員發現他們可以透過群組的整合，進行交易，發展規模經濟，大家
　因而獲益，社會可以就這樣形成。

K. When a person finds the knowledge of another person beneficial, there is a motivation to establish teacher student relationship.

　當一個人發現他可以從另一個人的知識得到好處，就會存在有形成一種師生關係的動機。

L.　When multiple persons find the knowledge of another person beneficial, there is a motivation to establish a group teaching.

　當許多人發現他們可以從另一個人的知識獲益，他們就會有動機促成群體教學的動機。

M. Each student in a teaching group has his own unique existing knowledge.

　一個教學群體中每個學生都有他自己的已有知識。

N. Due to trade and economies of scale, it is possible for a group member to achieve more than an individual alone.

　透過交易和規模經濟，有可能一個群體成員的收穫能超過他獨自一人努力的成就。

O. Group members trade part of their individual volition for their group rule.

　群體成員犧牲他們個人部分的自由意志以促成群體治理的目標。

P.　Each group member has his unique view regarding behaviors in the group.

　每個群體成員對於群體內的行為都會有他個人的獨特見解。

Q. Conflicted views often exist in a larger group.

　一個大的群體經常會有衝突的見解。

R. Each group has a conflict resolution mechanism.

　每個群體都有解決意見衝突的機制。

53. Principle of Stage

階段原理

Stage varies with the underlying person and time.

階段會隨著人的組成和時間而改變。

Corollaries to Stage Principle

成長階段原理的推論

A. Stage of a person correlates to the state of person at a given period.

一個人的階段與他在某一特定時間的狀況相互關聯。

B. Stage of a group varies with the underlying group and time.

一個群體的階段會隨著群體組成份子和時間而改變。

54. Principle of Growing Stage

成長階段原理

The learning capacity of a person in the growing stage is reduced by his time and capacity spent in growth, and his immaturity in communication skills.

一個人在成長階段的學習能力會因為他多花費在成長的時間和能量而降低，

Corollaries to Growing Stage Principle

成長階段原理的推論

A. A newborn baby has less capacity for learning and memory.

人類在新生兒階段還沒有足夠的能力學習與記憶。

B. An infant constructs his own memories after learning to differentiate various persons and objects.

幼兒期的人類在學會辨認不同的人和物品之後才開始建構他的記憶。

C. An infant constructs his own preferences after learning to distinguish various people and objects.

幼兒期的人類在學會區分不同的人和物品之後才開始建構他的偏好。

D. Improving a child's communication skills may increase the child's learning capacity.

改善一個小孩子的溝通技巧之後，就能夠增進他的學習能力。

E. Understanding a child's expressions and his existing knowledge is a guidance tool for a child's education.

了解一個小孩子的表情和他擁有的知識是教育一個小孩子必須的輔導工具。

F. Selection of information suitable for a child's existing knowledge is a guidance tool in a child's education.

選擇適合一個擁有某些知識的小孩子所能吸收的資訊是教育中兒童必須的輔導工具。

G. Introducing an appropriate mentor to a child is a tool.

將一個小孩交給是當的指導老師是重要的教育工具。

H. The more acceptable a mentor's existing knowledge is, the more the child may learn from the mentor.

一個指導老師所擁有的知識越容易讓小孩子接受，該小孩才會從他的指導老師學到越多。

I. Children like to play with and learn from other children close to their ages.

小孩子喜歡和跟他們年齡接近的小孩一起玩，也喜歡跟他們學習。

J. Children refresh their existing knowledge with creativities learned from other children.

小孩子用從其他小孩學來的創意更新他們已有的知識。

K. A mentor learns how to communicate with his mentee, refreshes and enhances his own existing knowledges.

一個指導老師會學會如何跟他指導的學生溝通，也能更新且增進他自己已有的知識。

L. Providing bridge information to connect a child's existing knowledge with a new information to be learned is a guidance tool for a child's education.

對兒童教育來說，提供橋段資訊使一個小孩子已有的知識得以連上他要
學習的新資訊是輔導的重要工具。

M. Dividing a larger piece of information into smaller pieces of information suitable for a child in growth stage is a guidance tool for a child's education.

對兒童教育來說，將一大堆的資訊分割成適合成長階段小孩子吸收的少量資訊是輔導的重要工具。

N. Arrange the order of a proper information sequence suitable for a child's existing knowledge is a guidance tool in a child's education.

對兒童教育來說，能將適當的資訊重新安排好順序使一個具有某些知識的小孩子能
方便吸收，這是輔導的重要工具。

O. Assistance for a child to fulfill his needs for food and attention may free up his capacity for learning.

幫助一個小孩子滿足他的食物和注意力需求，可以讓他有足夠的能力用來學習。

P. Guidance for a child to develop properly is a tool to increase the child's free capacity for learning.

能輔導一個小孩子適當地發展是讓小孩子能騰出更多能力學習的重要工具。

Q. Understanding and developing a child's senses and channel of information input is a guidance tool in child education.

了解並協助發展一個小孩子的感官知覺和吸收資訊的管道是兒童教育的重要輔導工具。

R. Understanding and supplying information to a child's learning environment is a guidance tool.

了解並提供資訊到一個小孩子的學習環境是重要的輔導工具。

S. Understanding a child's motives and motivating him is a guidance tool.

了解一個小孩子的動機，並能激勵他學習是重要的輔導工具。

T. Understanding and developing a child's learning skills is a guidance tool.

了解並協助發展一個小孩子的學習技能是重要的輔導工具。

U. Understanding a child's relationship and interactions with other people is a tool for an educator to develop guidance for a child's education.

了解一個小孩子與他人的關係，以及他和別人的互動，是幫助一個教育者發展兒
童教育中的輔導能力的主要工具。

V. Showing resources available for outreach is a guidance tool.

指出哪裡有可利用的資源好讓小孩子能擴展他們的知識是重要的輔導工具。

W. Building friendship and joining a group is a tool to expand a child's learning opportunity.

建立友誼和加入團體是拓展一個小孩子學習機會的重要工具。

X. Joining an organization gives a child an opportunity to learn under a structured environment.

加入組織會讓一個小孩子有機會在一個結構性的環境下學習。

Y. A pre-school teacher may adjust his curriculum according to the state of children from time to time.

一個幼兒園的老師可以根據小孩子的狀況隨時調整他的課程。

Z. When a class size is too large for a regular teacher to communicate effectively, it may be beneficial to have multiple teachers or divide the class into multiple classes.

如果一個班級太大無法使一般的老師能有效溝通,增加幾位老師或者將
班級分成幾個小班豆會有幫助的。

AA. When a class includes children of varied ages, mentorship may be a tool in a child's education.

對兒童教育來說,當一個班級包含不同年齡層的小孩子,引進指導老師當助理是可行的工具。

AB. Collaborative communication may be a useful tool in a class studying various topics.

引進協同教師到一個學習不同科目題材的班級可能是有用的工具。

55. Principle of Maintenance Stage
(Dedicated to Dr. George Forman on 12/24/2021)

維持階段原理 (獻給喬治福爾曼博士12/24/2021)

The learning ability of a person in maintenance stage is reduced by the time and functions spent to recover, restore, or maintain his body functions.

一個人在鞏固階段的學習能力會因為他多花費時間和機能在恢復,復原,或維護他的身體機能而降低。

Corollaries to Maintenance Stage Principle
維持階段原理的推論

A. An infant is a person in maintenance stage.

嬰兒是處於維持階段的人類。

B. The learning ability of an infant is reduced by infant's needs to grow, and the infant's immature communication skills.

一個嬰兒的學習能力會因為他必須維持成長,以及嬰兒的溝通能力不構成熟而減弱。

C. A sick student is in maintenance stage.

一位生病的學生也處於維持階段。

D. An adult with illness is in maintenance stage.

一位疾病纏身的成年人也處於維持階段。

E. A person taking remedial actions toward his disability is in maintenance stage.

一個人因為身體上有障礙而接受治療的人也處於維持階段。

F. A person in senior state is a person in maintenance stage.

一個高齡的人也處於維持階段。

G. The learning ability of a person in senior state is reduced by the person's physical degeneration, precautions taken, and the time and functions spent to recover, restore, or maintain his body functions.

一個高齡者的學習能力降低的原因是他的身體機能退化，採取預防措施過度小心，多花費時間和機能在恢復，復原，或維護他的身體機能。

    H. The learning ability of a person in maintenance stage is reduced, not impaired.

處於維持階段的人學習能力是降低，不是受到損害。

56. Principle of Open Communication
公開溝通原理

Although open communication may be made deliberately, it is most often used for convenience.

雖然公開溝通有可能是故意為之，他通常是因為方便才這麼做。

Corollaries to Open Communication Principle
公開溝通原理的推論

    A. A child may make confidential communications to someone whom he trusts.

一個小孩子可能只願意對他信任的人才進行秘密的溝通。

    B. A child may make private communications to close friends or relatives.

一個小孩子可能只對朋友或親人進行私底下溝通。

    C. A child often makes open communications due to limited communication skills.

一個小孩子可能因為溝通技巧受限才會做公開式的溝通。

    D. After a child becomes more sophisticated, he may also learn how to make deliberate open communications.

在變得比較成熟之後，一個小孩子才學會如何故意做公開式的溝通。

57. Principle of Over-Expressive
過度表達原理

A person who has strong desires to express his feeling frequently often make unnecessary expressions.

一個有強烈意圖要表白他感受的人常常會過度表達不必要的話。

Corollaries to Over-Expressive Principle
過度表達原理的推論

    A. A baby may cry as loud as he can to express his need of attention.

嬰兒可能會盡情大聲哭叫以表達他需要別人的注意。

    B. An unnecessary expression may be annoying or unwelcoming by the audience.

不必要的表達可能會讓聽眾覺得厭煩或不售旁人歡迎。

    C. When a child learns a new expression, he may be excited and overuse that expression.

當一個小孩子新學會一種新的表達方式，他或許會過度興奮，一再濫用該表達方式。

    D. Children often look like over-expressive people due to limited communication skills.

小孩子經常會像溝通技巧不足，過度表達的人們。

    E. An over-expressive person often is preoccupied with how to express himself and pay less attention to other matters.

一個經常過度表達的人過於專注如何表達自我，因而對別的事就比較不夠專注。

58. Outreach Motive Principle

擴大動機原理

A person's outreach motive varies with time.

一個人擴大動機的趨勢會隨時間而改變。

Corollary to Outreach Motive Principle

擴大動機原理的推論

Babies often cry for attention after showing signs of discomfort.

嬰兒常常在顯示不舒服的動作之後會用哭的方式進一步吸引注意。

59. Principle of Outreach

延伸原理

When a person feels he is not self-sufficient, it has a motive to outreach.

當一個人覺得他無法自給自足，就會出現延伸動作的動機。

60. Principle of Demand

要求原理

A person has a motive to request someone else's services or something not under his control for which he desires strongly; when the motive is strong enough, then the person will demand another person or party to fulfill his desires.

一個人會因為他無法控制他強烈渴求的東西，而產生動機要求別人的服務；當是項動機夠強烈，那個人就會要求另一個人或另一方滿足他的渴望。

Corollaries to Demand Principle

要求原理的推論

    A. Some children's outreach looks like demands due to limited communication skills.

       有些小孩的延伸動作看起來像要求，原因是這些小孩受限於他們溝通技巧的不足。

    B. Newly organized information from an outreach that fails to fulfill the original motive may turn into a new motive to make demands.

       來自延伸新整理出來的資訊無法滿足原來的動機，可能會轉變成提出要求的新動機。

    C. A demand can only be fulfilled with another party's cooperation

       一項要求只有得到另一方的合作，才得以滿足。

61. Principle of Conflict

衝突原理

There exists a conflict when the party to whom a demand is made does not fulfill the demand within a time frame.

當被要求的一方無法在期限內滿足該項要求，就會發生衝突。

Corollaries to Conflict Principle

衝突原理的推論

A. If a person desires to fulfill two incompatible motives, he has an internal conflict.

如果一個人期望達成兩項不相容的動機，他就會有自己的內在衝突。

B. If an organization receives two incompatible demands from members, the organization has an internal conflict.

如果一個組織收到成員兩項不相容的要求，該組織就會有本身的內在衝突。

C. When a demand is not fulfilled by the other party, an external conflict arises.

當另一方無法滿足某項要求，就會發生外在的衝突。

62. Partial Conflict Resolution Principle

部分解決衝突原理

Partial resolution may lead to a new confrontation, remain in status quo, or a total resolution.

衝突部份解決可能會引發一個新的衝突，維持現狀，或者得到完全的解決。

Corollaries to Partial Conflict Resolution Principle
部分解決衝突原理的推論

A. A counselor in students' disputes needs to balance the window of opportunity for conflict resolution against a total resolution.

協助學生解決紛爭的指導老師必須在解決衝突的機會窗口和完全解決之間取得平衡。

B. When a partial resolution is beneficial, a follow-up total resolution may be beneficial too.

當衝突部分解決使人獲益，隨之而來的完全解決也會有好處。

C. A party's position on a proposed partial resolution may become more aggressive or regressive over time.

隨著時間過去，有人提議出來的部份解決方案的一方可能會變得更好鬥，也有可能變得較收斂。

D. The parties need to weigh the window of opportunity for a partial resolution against a total resolution.

衝突的當事雙方必須在解決衝突的機會窗口和完全解決之間取得平衡。

E. A unilateral effort to resolve a group's differences with others in the conflict does not lead to a total resolution.

單邊的努力嘗試解決一個團體與其他人的差異問題所引起的衝突，並不會導致完全的解決。

63. Conflict Duration Principle

衝突持續期間原理

Conflict duration varies with time and the advancement in technology.

衝突持續期間隨著時間過去以及科技的進步而改變。

Corollaries to Conflict Duration Principle
衝突持續期間原理的推論

A. A third-party intervention may shorten or prolong an existing conflict.

第三方的介入或許能縮短或延長眼前的衝突。

B. A current technological innovation may shorten or prolong an existing conflict.

目前科技的創新也許能縮短或延長眼前的衝突。

64. Principle of Conflict Resolution
衝突解決原理

A conflict may be resolved by adjusting the demanding party and the demanded party's positions.

一樁衝突可能透過調整要求的一方和被要求的另一方的立場而得到解決。

Corollaries to Conflict Resolution Principle

衝突解決原理的推論

A. Adjustments of positions by the parties in a conflict follow the parties' learning or self-education processes.

衝突各方立場的調整往往來自各方學習或自我教育的過程。

B. Communications between the parties may serve as a mutual education.

衝突雙方的溝通可以當作互相給對方的教育。

C. A total resolution may vary with time and the environments.

衝突的完全解決會隨時間的過去和環境的變化而改變。

D. The parties may use a window of opportunity for conflict resolution.

衝突雙方可以利用衝突解決的機會窗口來解決衝突。

E. People often self-educate and resolve their motive conflicts by:

人們常常通過自我教育並透過下列的方法解決他們動機上的衝突：

    i. seeking advice from others;
    尋求別人的忠告意見；

    ii. giving up one or more of his motives;
    放棄其中的一項動機；

    iii. scheduling the fulfillments in different time frames;
    安排在不同的時程滿足要求；

    iv. shifting priorities to other objectives;
    轉移優先順序給其他的目標；

    v. putting off the fulfillments for future resolution;
    延緩滿足要求等到未來再解決；

    vi. living with the conflicts; or
    與衝突共存；

    vii. suffering consequences of the conflicts.
    承受衝突的後續苦果。

F. Organizations often resolve their internal conflicts by one or more of the following ways:

組職通常以下列方法之一或多個方法解決組織內的衝突：

    i. fulfilling only one or neither of the demands;
    只滿足一個或者零個要求；

    ii. scheduling the fulfillments in different time frames;
    安排在不同的時程滿足要求；

    iii. adjusting demands to make them compatible to each other;
    調整要求使它們能夠互相相容；

    iv. shifting priorities to other objectives;

將優先順序轉移給其他的目標；

v. putting off the fulfillments for future resolution;

延緩滿足要求等到未來再解決；

vi. seeking helps from a third party;

尋求第三方協助處理；

vii. accepting the co-existence of conflicting issues; or

接受矛盾的事情同時存在的事實；

viii. suffering from damages, divisions, splits, or destructions to the organization.

承受衝突的後續苦果，如損害、分開對立、分裂、或對組織造成破壞。

G. External conflicts are often resolved in one or more of the following ways:

人們通常以下列方法之一或多個方法解決外在衝突：

i. finding that some of the underlying motives of their demands are no longer in existence;

發現某些要求的背後動機已經不再存在；

ii. some demands will not be enforced;

有些要求不會被執行；

iii. some demands are being put off for future resolutions;

延緩滿足有些要求等到未來再解決；

iv. some demands may be fulfilled with alternatives;

有些要求改以其他方式實施；

v. some demands may be put on hold for negotiations;

有些要求暫時被擱置另行協商；

vi. the demands may be satisfied through a negotiated resolution;

雙方同意找第三方仲裁；

vii. the parties bring themselves to a third-party arbitration; or

雙方同意找第三方仲裁；

viii. the parties fight one another.

ix. 雙方互相攻擊。

H. Social responsibility education, if properly administrated, may reduce potential social conflicts in the future.

如果處置得當，社會責任教育或許能在未來減輕潛在的社會衝突。

I. The Principle of Act in Time applies to conflict resolution.

及時行動原則可用來解決衝突。

J. Early childhood education provides the best opportunity for prevention of future conflicts.

早期的兒童教育提供最好的機會預防未來的衝突。

65. Principle of a Window of Opportunity for Conflict Resolution
解決衝突機會窗口原理

A window of opportunity for conflict resolution exists when the parties take the window of opportunity for learning to study possible resolutions and adjust their positions.

如果起衝突的雙方利用機會窗口學習研究可能解決方案，並調整雙方的立場，那麼解決衝突的機會窗口就會存在。

Corollaries to Window of Opportunity for Conflict Resolution Principle
解決衝突機會窗口原理的推論

A. Each party's position in a conflict varies with time.

各方的立場會隨時間過去而改變。

B. Both window of opportunity for learning and window of opportunity for conflict resolution vary with time.

學習的機會窗口和解決衝突的機會窗口都會隨時間而改變。

C. Each party in a conflict should take its window of opportunity to learn the parties' positions and intentions so that it may reevaluate whether or how its demands can be fulfilled.

衝突各方應該利用機會窗口熟悉雙方的立場與意圖，如此一來，雙方才會有機會
重新評估是否且如何能滿足要求。

D. The Principle of Act in Time applies to conflict resolution.

及時行動原則可用來解決衝突。

E. When a country receives another country's ultimatum, there is a window for resolution.

當一個國家收到另一個國家的最後通牒，還是會有機會窗口解決問題。

F. The action of issuing an ultimatum signifies the gravity of the conflict and the approaching end of window for resolution.

採取發出最後通牒的行動代表衝突的嚴重性，那表示解決問題的機會窗口已經接近關閉。

G. The window of opportunity for conflict resolution may decrease in the future due to advancement in technology.

因為科技的進步，未來面臨解決衝突的機會窗口也許會減少。

66. Principle of Setback

挫敗原理

When a party realizes that its demand is not attainable, the party has a setback.

當某一方知道它的要求無法達成，它就只好承認挫敗。

Corollaries to Setback Principle

挫敗原理的推論

A. A setback may turn into a motive to search for the causes of the setback.

一次挫敗可能會轉化成意圖尋找挫敗原因的動機。

B. A person's newly organized information from a setback may turn into an adjustment to the person's or party's original motive.

一個人從挫敗新學到的資訊可能會使這個人或團體轉而調整原來的動機。

C. If a person's motivational underlying original demand has not been changed, a newly organized information from the setback may turn into a new motive for alternative ways to fulfill its desires.

如果一個人原來由背後的動機所策動的要求沒有改變，那麼從挫敗學到的新資訊可能會轉化成尋求
另外的方法以滿足期望的新動機。

D. A setback may create a sense of resentment.

挫敗可能會產生厭惡感。

E. A setback may cause a person to take a holdback position on some issues.

挫敗可能會讓一個人決定對某些問題採取裹足不前的立場。

67. Principle of Giving

贈與原則

A party confers outright benefits to another.

一方將利益給予另一方的行為。

Corollaries to Giving Principle

贈與原理的推論

    A. A partial gift is made which equals to the difference between the value of gift deducted by the value received in exchange of the gift.

    一件禮物的價值扣掉收到交換禮物的價值所產生的差額就叫做不完全的禮物。

    B. Things under a giving party's control are not an outright gift.

    仍然受到送禮者控制的東西不能算做是不折不扣的完全禮物。

68. Principle of Negotiation

協商原理

When the first party desires the second party to change position, the first party may reach out to the second party for negotiation.

當第一方希望第二方改變立場，第一方可能會主動找第二方協商。

Corollaries to Negotiation Principle

協商原理的推論

    A. An underlying motive for a negotiation to reach an agreement is a common ground among the parties.

    一項追求協議的協商的背後動機就是雙方的共同之處。

    B. "The benefits outweigh the costs" is often a party's motive to seek a common ground.

    「獲益超過成本」常常是一方要尋求共同之處的動機。

69. Principle of Holdback

裹足不前原理

The newly organized information from a setback may turn into a motive to hold back.

從挫敗新習得的資訊可能會轉化成裹足不前的動機。

Corollaries to Holdback Principle

裹足不前原理的推論

    A. A child in holdback position might be intimidated by previous setbacks.

    有裹足不前立場的小孩子或許會被以前的挫敗嚇到了。

    B. A prolonged period of holdback state may lead to introversion.

    長時間維持裹足不前的狀態可能會使小孩子的個性變內向。

70. Principle of Incentive
誘因原理

An incentive may be a motive for a party to act.

誘因可能是某一方採取行動的動機。

Corollaries to Incentive Principle
誘因原理的推論

A. An incentive may bring a person out of holdback state.

某個誘因有可能將一個裹足不前的小孩子帶出來。

B. Repetitive attention to an incentive may lead to a motivation focused on the incentive itself.

反覆注意到某個誘因可能激勵專注在該誘因本身的動機。

71. Principle of Competition
競爭原理

A party enters a competition with others for the purpose of winning rewards associated with the winning of the competition.

某一方為了贏得透過競爭優勝才能取得的獎金就必須和別人競爭。

Corollaries to Competition Principle
競爭原理的推論

A. Each party in a competition has its own objectives or rewards associated with the competition, which may or may not be limited to the official prize of the competition.

競賽各方都有參加競賽各自想達成的目標和想獲得的獎金，那些目標和獎金可能受限於也可能不受限於競賽所公布的獎項或金額。

B. Participation in a competition may serve as a motivation for the participant to become better.

參加競賽可能被參與者當作是追求進步的動機。

C. A conflict may arise when one participant demands another participant to act (or not act) in a certain way.

當一位競爭者要求另一位競爭者只能做或者不能做某種動作，那就會產生衝突。

72. Principle of Association
聯誼原理

People associate themselves for a joint purpose.

人們會為了某個共同目的而參加聯誼。

Corollaries to Association Principle
聯誼原理的推論

A. Each association member's support of the joint purpose varies with time.

每個聯誼社團的成員對於社團共同宗旨的支持度會隨時間而變化。

B. The joint purpose of the association as well as the members may vary with time.

聯誼社的共同宗旨和社團成員會隨時間而變化。

73. Principle of Sharing
共享原理

A person gives some of his resources, works, services, and performance to someone of his choice.

一個人會將他的部分資源，工作，服務和成就與他所選擇的人分享。

Corollaries to Sharing Principle
共享原理的推論

A. People often share things with other people who they love.

人們常常將他們的事務跟他們所喜愛的人分享。

B. A team member may share his resources and work to other team members who work with him.

一個團隊成員可能會跟和他一起工作的其他團隊成員分享他的資源和工作。

C. Sharing team resources on need basis may impact their teamwork positively.

根據需求分享團隊資源肯定會對團隊的聯合作業產生好的影響。

D. Sharing too many resources may overwhelm other team members with wastes and the unnecessary burden of managing the extra resources.

分享過多資源可能會讓其他團隊成員一下子承受不了，造成太多浪費，為了管理多餘資源，也會造成他們不必要的負擔。

74. Principle of Round Robin
環狀溝通原理

A round robin communication lets each team member take turns for presentation.

一個環狀溝通模式讓每個團隊成員輪流發表意見。

Corollaries to Round Robin Principle
環狀溝通原理的推論

A. A round robin gives each team member an equal opportunity for participation.

一個環狀溝通模式讓每個團隊成員輪流發表意見。

B. A round robin may be effective for a small team but may be cumbersome for a larger team.

一個環狀溝通模式對小團隊來說可能效果不錯，但是對大團隊就可能很累贅。

75. Principle of Cross-Communication
橫跨溝通原理

Cross-communication allows a team member to communicate directly with another person or a bunch of people.

跨部門溝通模式讓團隊成員可以跟一個人或一票人直接溝通。

Corollaries to Cross-Communication Principle
橫跨溝通原理的推論

A. A Cross-communication allows a team member to avoid waiting time for other team members' presentation in a round robin.

橫跨溝通模式讓一個團隊成員可以避免浪費等待時間，直接跟其他團隊成員溝通。

B. A team leader needs to manage cross-communication if it is used; the cross-communication may create chaos otherwise when more than one team member tries to make presentation simultaneously.

如果採用橫跨溝通模式，一個團隊領導有必要管理好橫跨溝通；當超過一個團隊成員嘗試同時發表意見，橫跨溝通就會造成一片混亂。

C. Public speech may be an effective method of cross-communication.

公開演說會是一種有效的橫跨溝通模式。

D. Publication may be an effective method of cross-communication.

出版會是一種有效的橫跨溝通模式。

E. Broadcasting may be an effective method of cross-communication.

廣播會是一種有效的橫跨溝通模式。

F. Voting may an effective method of a cross-communication.

投票會是一種有效的橫跨溝通模式。。

76. Principle of Structured Organization

結構性組織原理

When an organization has a large number of members, it is beneficial for the organization to restructure itself into several divisions.

如果一個組織有許多成員，將該組織重新改組成許多分支，組織立刻就會獲益。

Corollaries to Structured Organization Principle
結構性組織原理的推論

A. Division of works may be assigned along the divisions of a structured organization.

事務的分工可以依循組織的分支結構來分配工作。

B. Channel of commands may be implemented in a structured organization.

命令要求的溝通管道可以按組織的結構依序執行。

C. Ranking and levels may be established in a structured organization.

結構性組織有利於建構具有層次與順序的組織。

D. Vertical communications, horizontal communications, and collaborative communications may be implemented for effective operation of a structured organization.

垂直溝通，水平溝通，以及協調式溝通都可以在結構性組織內實施，組織機能也能因而有效操作。

77. Training Principle

訓練原理

A training program must be appropriate to the trainee.

訓練的方案計畫都要能適合受訓者的需要。

Corollaries to Training Principle

訓練原理的推論

A. The same training program appropriate to a trainee at one point of time may not be appropriate at another point of time.

同樣的訓練方案計畫某個時期對受訓者合適，換個時間點它可能就不見得合適。

B. The same training program appropriate to one trainee may not be appropriate to another trainee.

同樣的訓練方案計畫對某個受訓者可能合適，換個受訓者它可能就不見得洽當。

C. When a training program is too large for a trainee, segmentation of the training program may be beneficial for the trainee.

如果某個訓練方案計畫對一個受訓者過於龐大，將該計畫分割成幾個階段
可能會對受訓者的吸收比較有用。

78. Principle of Team

團隊原理

A group of people are organized for the purpose of performing specific tasks together.

一群為了一起完成特定工作的目的而被組織起來的人組成一個團隊。

79. Principle of Teamwork

團隊合作原理

Teamwork is the collective achievements of all team members.

團隊聯合作業指的是所有團隊成員工作的總合成就。

Corollaries to Teamwork Principle

團隊合作原理的推論

A. Each member of a team performs a part of the teamwork assigned to him.

每個團隊成員負責完成指派給他團隊聯合作業工作的一部份。

B. Team members and the assignment of tasks vary with time.

團隊成員以及任務的分派會隨時間而改變。

C. Specialization may improve the effectiveness of a teamwork.

專人專責的分工可以改進團隊聯合作業的效率。

D. The foundation of teamwork is the existence of some common existing knowledge and agreements among the team members.

團隊聯合作業奠基於一些已知共有知識以及團隊成員協議共識的存在。

E. Childhood education sets the stage for all education that follows throughout a person's life. It is important to guide children with common educational background and prepare them for teamwork later in life.

兒童教育架好了一個人長大以後所有教育的舞台，重要的是，引導小孩子小時候就具備相同的教育背景，
讓他們準備好能擔負起後來一生團隊聯合作業份內的工作。

F. Time is of essence. It is crucial to provide common educational background in childhood.

時間的因素最重要，在孩童時期就提供他們共通的教育背景非常關鍵。

G. Specialized education may be appropriate in higher education.

特定的專業教育較合適在高等教育階段訓練。

80. Principle of Team Leader
團隊領導原理

A team is led by a team leader at a given time. A team leader may be a person, a team, or organizations co-leadership in a larger team.

一個團隊在某一時期會由團隊首腦來領導該團隊。團隊領導可能是一個人、一個小組、
或一個大團體裡的組織共同領導。

Corollaries to Team Leader Principle
團隊領導原理的推論

A. The vision and efficiency of the team's leadership may impact the team's performance.

團隊領導的遠見和效率會影響到該團隊的表現。

B. Team leadership may lead the team into peace or conflicts.

團隊領導有可能帶給一個團隊安寧祥和，也可能將一個團隊帶往衝突混亂的狀態。

C. The efficiency of communications between a team leader and the team members may impact the teamwork.

團隊領導與團隊成員之間的溝通是否有效會影響到團隊的整體作業。

D. The efficiency of communications among the team members may impact the teamwork.

團隊成員之間的溝通是否有效會影響到團隊的整體作業。

E. Team members, teamwork, and team leader may vary with time.

團隊成員，團隊的整體作業，團隊領導都會隨時間而改變。

F. Parents may be a team leader.

父母親或許也是一個團隊的領導。

G. An example of organizations acting in co-leadership is the government, where different branches work together to serve the nation.

政府機構就是一個組織共同領導的例子，政府不同部門共同合作服務整個國家。

H. Peaceful succession of a team's leadership is critical to the team's ongoing concern.

一個團隊領導的權力和平轉移對於該團隊人人關切的進行中工作能夠無縫接軌非常關鍵。

I. It is the team and the team leader's responsibility to utilize prudently the resources of the team for the benefit of the team.

謹慎利用一個團隊的資源已謀求團隊的整體利益是團隊也是團隊領導的責任。

J. A team leader's recognition of the state of each team member is critical to effective team communication.

一個團隊領導能夠體會每個團隊成員的狀況對於有效的團隊溝通非常關鍵。

K. A team and its members are continually educated by the constant changes in the universe.

一個團隊和它的成員繼續不斷地從世界不停的改變得到教育。

L. Appropriate adjustments may be beneficial to a team and its members from time to time.

經常做適當的調整都會使一個團隊和它的成員獲得好處。

M. One of the team's most crucial potential benefits is the team's relationship to its environments, including but not limited to the relationship with other groups in the environments.

一個團隊與它周遭環境的關係，包括但不限於它跟同一環境中的其他團隊之間的關係，
是該團隊最重要的潛在利益之一。

N. Training team members may improve team performance.

訓練團隊成員可以改善整個團隊的表現。

O. Team members' training in total person approach to human relationship is the most critical factor for a team's long-term survival.

將團隊成員訓練成一個個與其他人類保持關係的全人教育是一個團隊能夠永續生存最關鍵的因素。

P. Specialized training for team members may contribute to the team's effectiveness.

將團隊成員訓練成具備專門技能的人員可能會對該團隊的效率很有貢獻。

81. Adjustment Principle
調整原理

Adjustment is an educated change to a prior establishment.

調整指的是將已建立好的機構根據知識經驗所做的改變。

Corollaries to Adjustment Principle
調整原理的推論

A. A person may update and adjust his existing knowledge.

一個人可能會更新和調整它現有的知識。

B. An inappropriate adjustment may not be beneficial and may worsen an existing condition.

不洽當的調整可能沒有好處，甚至於會使現有的條件更為惡化。

C. A plan may be adjusted along the course of execution.

一項計畫也許會在執行過程中逕行調整。

D. Rehabilitations may contribute to adjustments of a person's physical functions.

復健工作或許會調整一個人的身體機能。

E. Medications may be used to adjust a person's physical condition.

藥物治療也許會用來調整一個人的身體狀況。

F. Surgeries may be beneficial to remove or repair damaged or injured body parts.

外科手術對割除或修復受損或受傷的身體部位會有幫助。

G. In some cases, a society may find healing by separating some people from society for a period.

在某些情況下，一個社會可能會透過將一些人從社會上隔離一段時期而找到療癒效果。

H. It may be more efficient to take corrective actions than to spend a person's limited capacity on resentment.

採取行動矯正問題比起花費個人有限的能量在怨恨別人要來得有效率多了。

I. Corrective actions may be positive or negative.

矯正動作可能是正面的，也可能是負面的。

J. Examples of positive corrective action include: to recover from a setback; to find out the cause of the setback; to avoid similar setback in the future; to review and improve the process of corrective actions; and to review and plan for guidance and resources needed for future corrective actions.

正面的矯正行動的例子包括：設法從挫敗中恢復過來；設法找出造成挫敗的原因；設法避免以後再產生挫敗；設法重新檢視並改善矯正行動的過程；設法重新檢視並規畫輔導和未來矯正行動所需的資源。

K. Guidance and education may contribute to a person's adjustments.

輔導與教育可能對一個人的調適會有貢獻。

L. The act in time approach may be critical to the effectiveness of the adjustments.

及時行動的作法對於調整是否有效果可能很關鍵。

Glossary
語彙表

Action

行動

Doing something.
做某件事。

Association

聯誼會；學會

A group of people organized for a joint purpose.
一些有共同目的的人所組成的群組

Attachment

親近感

When one relies emotionally on another party, he is said to have an attachment.
當某人感情上仰賴另一個人，他與對方的親近感油然而生。

Biased Condition

使產生偏差的條件

A set of conditions which excludes some relevant factors in an experiment.
造成實驗中一些相關因素被排除掉的條件。

Body Function Curve

身體功能發展曲線

A multi-dimensional function which denotes a person's emotional, spiritual, and bodily conditions, organ functions and senses, such as sensory functions, motor functions, organ functions, memory functions, analytical functions, emotion functions, chemical functions, immune mechanism, defense mechanism, tiredness, sickness, restoration functions, growth, aging, bonding, and connection, etc.
用以表示一個人的感情，精神，以及身體狀況，器官機能與各種感覺的一種多面向功能，譬如感官功能，運動功能，器官機能，記憶功能，分析功能，感情作用，化學作用，免疫機制，防衛機制，疲憊狀態，疾病狀態，恢復功能，成長，老化，牽掛，和連結等等。

Bond Relationship ("Bond")

人際關係(結合)

A simple bond relationship ("bond") exists when a person trusts another person on a particular matter for a particular period.
當某人在某一期間信賴另一個人某一特定事項，他們之間就存有一種單純的人際關係(結合)。

Collaborative Communication

協調式溝通

Ways of communication to provide workflows to create experiences for disparate teams inside or outside a structured organization.
協調式溝通指的是促使結構性組織內部與外部非常相異的團體能夠透過工作上的協商創造溝通的經驗。

Comfortable Zone

舒適圈

How an individual chooses to act in order to makes himself feel well at a given point of time.
個人在某一特定時間選擇如何行動好讓他自己感覺良好的環境。

Communication

溝通

When information is transmitted back and forth between individuals or parties.
不同的個人或群體之間來來往往的訊息的交換。

Competition

競爭

An event in which two or more participants present their works or performances for comparison.
雙方或多方各自發表他們的工作成果或各方的表現以供比較的事件。

Confidence

信心

A person's feeling that he possesses the capability to handle a task at a given point of time.

一個人覺得自己擁有在某一時候處理某項工作的本事。

Conflict

衝突

The condition where more than one motivation or desires cannot co-exist without modification.

超過一個動機或願望如果沒有經過修改無法共存的情況。

Conflict Duration

衝突持續期間

The period begins from creation of the differences among the parties and ends with a total resolution.

從當事各方產生異議開始到差異圓滿解決為止的持續期間。

Conflict Resolution

衝突解決

A process to resolve the conflict.

解決衝突的過程。

Connection

關聯

The result of mutual bonds between two parties.

雙方因交際而形成的相互關係。

Critical State of Existing Knowledge

知識形成的臨界點

When a person's existing knowledge reaches a minimum condition beyond which the existing knowledge may have positive impact on a learning target.

一個人現有的知識最少要累積到某一程度，使得它會對學習標的產生正面影響的臨界門檻。

Critical State for Learning

學習的關鍵狀況

When a person's state reaches a minimum condition beyond which the person may have an opportunity for positive learning

一個人的狀況最少要進步到某一程度，使得他能得到正面學習機會的關鍵狀況。

Demand

要求

A party's preemptory request to another party.

一方對另一方的嚴正請求。

Desire

願望

A strong motivation to obtain something or services.

欲求得到某物或某項服務的強烈動機。

Dominant State

顯性狀態

The part of a person's state which is most influential or noticeable at a given point of time.

一個人在某一特定時候最具有影響力或最引起別人注意的狀態。

Education

教育

A person's learning from available resources.

一個人從可利用的資源所獲得的學習。

Education Goal

教育目標

The objectives of an education.

Educational Tool ("Tool")

教育工具

Information, instruments, curriculum, programs, ideas, algorithms, organizations, environments, rules, laws, and regulations, etc. which can be used to help education.

可以用來幫助教育的資訊，器材，課程，想法，演算法，組織，環境，規則，法條，以及規章等。

Existing Knowledge

已有的知識

Organized information which is either retrieved from a person's long-term memory or retained in the person's temporary memory at a specific time.

從一個人的長期記憶或某個時候還保留在他的短暫記憶所取得的系統知識。

External Conflict

外在的衝突

A conflict involving another party.

牽扯到另一方的衝突。

Free Capacity

可供自由使用的能力。

A person's capability to perform tasks of his own volition at a given point of time.

一個人在某一特定時候自願完成工作的能力。

Giving

贈與

When one party confers benefits to another.

一方將利益給予另一方的行為。

Gross Capacity

整體能力

A person's total capacity at a given point of time.

一個人在某一特定時候的能力總和。

Group

群體

Two or more persons classified together as a Group.

被歸屬於同一類的兩個或兩個以上的人合稱為一群體。

Group Member

群體成員

A person in the group.

群體中的一個人。

Growing Stage

成長階段

When a person utilizes a substantial part of his time and functions to grow and develop his body functions.

當一個人使用大部分的時間以及各種功能讓自己成長，發展身體機能能的階段。

Guidance

輔導

Assistance leading to a targeted education and avoiding unintended consequence.

能導致目標教育，避免造成非故意後果的輔助。

Hold Back

裹足不前

When a person does not want to express himself at a given point of time.

一個人不願意在某一特定時候表達自己的想法。

Horizontal Communication

橫向水平溝通

Communications between two persons of the same or similar level or ranking in a structured organization.

在結構性組織具有相同或類似水準或階級的兩個人之間的溝通。

Ideal Education

理想的教育

When all predetermined education goals have been attained with 100% effectiveness and no unintended information learned in the process.

理想的教育指的是所有預定教育目標100%全部達成，而且在過程中沒有任何非計畫中的資訊被學習到。

Incentive

誘因

Material or services designed to induce or enhance a person's motivation.

誘因指的是設計以誘發或加強某個人動機的材料或服務。

Information

訊息

Any idea or matter which could be detected or learned in any way.

可以用任何方式偵測或學習得到的想法或事情。

Information Environment

資訊環境

All information to which a person is exposed at a specific time.

某一特定時候一個人所接觸到的所有資訊的總和。

Information Input

訊息輸入

All information received by a person, either through internal and external sensory systems or retrieved from his long-term memory.

一個人所接收到的所有資訊，包括透過內在與外在感官知覺系統吸收，或從他的長期記憶擷取者。

Information Management

資訊管理

Preliminary selection, temporary retention, pattern recognition, and functions initiation based on interpretations of the information.

初步選擇，暫存，模式識別，根據資訊闡釋啟用功能。

Internal Conflict

內在衝突

A conflict within a person or within a group.

個人內在衝突或群體內的衝突。

Intentional Misinformation

刻意傳播訊息錯誤

Incorrect information with the purpose of misleading a targeted audience.

傳播不正確的資訊，目的在誤導特定的受眾。

Learning Path

學習途徑

The path or the collection of all events for a person to learn a piece of information.

個人學習某一訊息所需的所有事件的途徑與收集。

Long-Term Memory

長期記憶

Organized information that is stored in a person's brain, or other parts of his body.

整理過的資訊儲存到一個人腦部或身體其他部位。

Maintenance Stage

維持階段

The state of a person when utilizes a substantial part of his time and functions to recover, restore, or maintain his body functions.

一個人利用大部分時間與身心功能以便復原，儲藏，或維持他身體機能的階段。

Mental State
心理狀況

A person's mental state and conditions, such as intellectual, rational, cognitive, spirits, beliefs, etc.
一個人的心理狀況與條件，如智慧的，理性的，認知的，精神的，信仰的各種狀況。

Misinformation
錯誤訊息

Transmission of incorrect information.
不正確訊息的傳佈。

Motivation
驅策力量

A reason to act in a particular way.
驅策個人採取特定方式行動的力量。

Motive
動機

An inclination.
某種行為傾向。

Multiple Distances
保持多種距離

Multiple distances relationship ("multiple distances") exists when a person has multiple distancing at a particular point of time.
當一個人在某一特定時間與人維持多種距離時，保持多種距離關係(多種距離關係)就會存在。

Negotiation
協商

Two or more persons communicating with each other for the purpose of making an agreement.
兩人或多人之間互相溝通，目的在達成協議。

Newly Organized Information
新整理的資訊

Organized information a part of which is not in existing knowledge.
整理出來的資訊並非既有知識的一部分。

Non-Priority Educational Condition ("Non-Priority Condition")
非優先的教育條件(非優先條件)

The dimensions or conditions of an education environment which are not chosen for considerations are called non-priority educational conditions.
並未特別挑選的某一教育環境面向和條件稱之為非優先教育條件。

Open communication
開放式溝通

When a person communicates with another person without limitation on its further retransmission.
當一個人與另一人溝通時，對進一步再轉發並未設限的溝通。

Over-Expressive
過度表達

A characteristic of a person who often makes unnecessary expression.
一個人特性上經常有做非必要表達的傾向。

Party
當事人

A person, an association, an organization, or any group of people who has a representative.
有代表人的個人，同事，組織，或任何群組。

Outreach
延伸

A party's efforts to communicate with another party.
當事一方要跟另一方溝通的努力嘗試。

Outreach Motive

往外延伸的動機

A person's reason for communicating with another person.

一個人要跟另一人溝通的理由。

Partial Conflict Resolution ("Partial Resolution")

衝突部份解決(部份解決)

A confrontational or a recessive conflict has been turned into another recessive conflict.

某個衝突或衰退衝突轉成另一個衰退衝突。

Perfect Educational Condition ("Perfect Condition")

完美的教育環境

When all conditions of an educational environment are met to their full potential.

當一個教育環境的所有條件都符合可以讓學習者的潛能充分發揮。

Physical State

身體狀況

A person's bodily state and conditions, such as arms, legs, heart, brain, etc.

一個人身體的狀況和條件,譬如手臂,腿部,心臟,頭腦等各部位的狀況。

Potential of a Learner ("Potential")

學習者的潛能(潛能)

An educational potential of a learner, also called a potential, is the existence of a reasonable probability for the learner to attain a targeted goal of education.

一個學習者的教育潛能,又簡稱為潛能,指的是學習者具有合理的可能性會達到預期的教育目標。

Priority Educational Condition ("Priority Condition")

優先順序教育條件(優先條件)

When only some dimensions or conditions of an education environment are chosen for consideration.

只挑選教育環境的部分面相或條件作為考量的時候。

Private Communication

私人溝通

A person's communication with someone who is close to him.

一個人跟接近他的人溝通稱之為私人溝通。

Prize

獎項

An award for winning in a competition

贏得某項競賽所獲得的獎品。

Recessive State

衰退狀況

The part of a person's state that may be overshadowed by the person's dominant state.

比一個人的巔峰狀態要來得失色的部份狀況。

Search

蒐尋

A person's efforts to collect additional information.

一個人嘗試收集額外資訊所做的努力。

Self Sufficiency

自給自足

The condition of a person thinking that all his needs can be fulfilled by himself alone.

一個人認為他的所有需求他都能獨力達成的情況。

Set Back

挫敗

A person walks back some or all his previous demands.

一個人陷入某種狀況,被迫重新考量以前部分或所有的需求。

Sharing

分享

    When a party gives some of his resources, works, or performance to another.

    當事一方將他的部分資源，工作，或成果給予另一方的動作。

Simple Distancing Relationship ("Distancing")

單純保持距離關係(保持距離)

    When a person distrusts another person on a particular matter for a particular period.

    當一個人不相信另一個人在某一特定時間就某事所持的觀點。

Stage

階段

    A characteristic of a person standing out during a specific period.

    一個人在某一特定時期所表現出來的特性。

Stage of a Group

群體的階段

    A statistic of similar or common characteristics of a group at a specific period.

    一個群體的成員在某一特定時期所呈現出來相似的或共有的特性。

State of a Group

群體的狀況

    A collection of the states of the group members.

    一個群體所有成員狀況的集合。

Strong Bond

堅固的人際關係

    A long-lasting simple bond or multiple bonds.

    長遠持久的單純人際關係或多重的關係。

Strong Distancing Relationship

強烈的保持距離關係

    The moving away or against another person's wish due to a simple or multiple distancing.

    因為單純的或多重的保持距離措舉而與另一人保持距離關係(遠離對方或違背對方意思的行為)。

Structured Organization

結構性的組織

    A group of which the members in the group are divided or subdivided into various subgroups or divisions in accordance with the group defined levels, rankings, and organizational structure.

    根據一個群體所定義的階層，位階與組織結構而將該群體區分成或細分為各式各樣的分部或分處。

Team

團隊

    A group of people organized to work together.

    一群人因為在一起工作而組成的團隊。

Team Leader

團隊領導

    A person who is in charge of the team for the purpose of achieving their goals.

    領導一個團隊一起完成他們工作目標的負責人。

Teamwork

團隊工作

    Work conducted by a team in which the members are divided into a smaller subgroups and work on their respectively assigned parts of the work in collaboration with other team members.

    一個團隊將成員分成較小的群組，然後將工作分派給負責不同工作的小團隊成員，要求他們與其他的團隊成員合作，一起完成團隊整體的工作目標。

Total Conflict Resolution ("Total Resolution")

衝突全部解決(全部解決)

    When a confrontational or a recessive conflict has been eliminated, all parties' differences regarding the issue have been reconciled, and will not be a cause of another conflict in the future.

    某個衝突或衰退衝突已被消除，對議題所持的差異各方已經得到折衷達成協議，將來也不會引發另一個衝突。

Trammel State

阻礙狀態

When a person's state shows that the person's learning efficiency are significantly less effective than average person's.

當一個人的狀況顯示他的學習效率比起一般人的學習效率大打折扣，他就是處於一種阻礙狀態。

Training

訓練

A process of targeted learning.

一個有目標的學習過程。

Transmission

傳播

When a party conveys information to another party.

當某一方將訊息傳達給另一方的過程。

Vertical Communication

垂直溝通

A direct communication between two persons of different level or ranking in a structured organization.

由群體組織架構中不同階層或位階的兩個人之間的垂直溝通。

Window of Opportunity for Conflict Resolution

解決衝突的機會窗口

The time frame within which a conflict may be resolved without use of force.

未動用外力就能解決衝突的時間框架範圍。

Window of Opportunity for Learning

學習的機會窗口

A time interval when a person is in a critical or more suitable state for learning.

適合一個人學習的關鍵狀況所在的時間間隔。

國家圖書館出版品預行編目資料

教育原理／宋武峰（Donald W. Sung）作. --
初版.--臺中市：白象文化事業有限公司，2023.3
　　　面；　公分
中英對照
譯自：Principles of education
ISBN 978-626-7253-21-2（精裝）
1.CST: 兒童教育　2.CST: 教育理論
523　　　　　　　　　　　　111020581

教育原理

作　　者	宋武峰（Donald W. Sung）
	翻印許可請洽：donsung3@gmail.com
譯　　者	宋武峰（Donald W. Sung）
校　　對	宋武峰（Donald W. Sung）
發 行 人	張輝潭
出版發行	白象文化事業有限公司
	412台中市大里區科技路1號8樓之2（台中軟體園區）
	出版專線：（04）2496-5995　　傳真：（04）2496-9901
	401台中市東區和平街228巷44號（經銷部）
	購書專線：（04）2220-8589　　傳真：（04）2220-8505
出版編印	林榮威、陳逸儒、黃麗穎、水邊、陳媁婷、李婕
設計創意	張禮南、何佳諠
經紀企劃	張輝潭、徐錦淳、廖書湘
經銷推廣	李莉吟、莊博亞、劉育姍、林政泓
行銷宣傳	黃姿虹、沈若瑜
營運管理	林金郎、曾千熏
印　　刷	基盛印刷工場
初版一刷	2023 年 3 月
定　　價	360 元

白象文化　印書小舖　出版・經銷・宣傳・設計
www.ElephantWhite.com.tw　自費出版的領導者　購書 白象文化生活館